AF746498

Name

Teacher

School

Are you ready to write?

Posture

Ensure your feet are flat on the floor and you are sitting well back in the chair.

Paper position

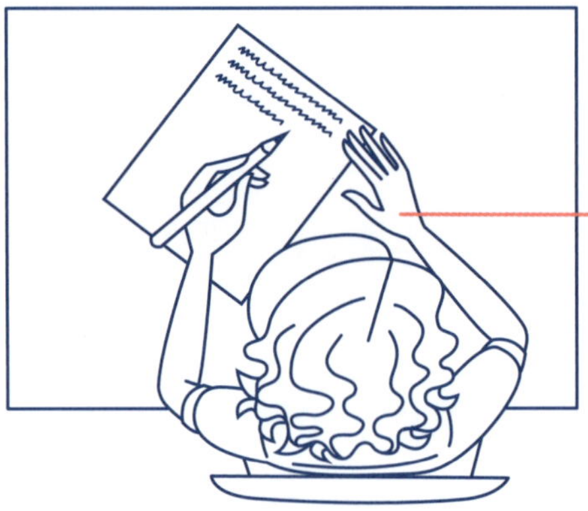

Hold the paper with your non-writing hand.

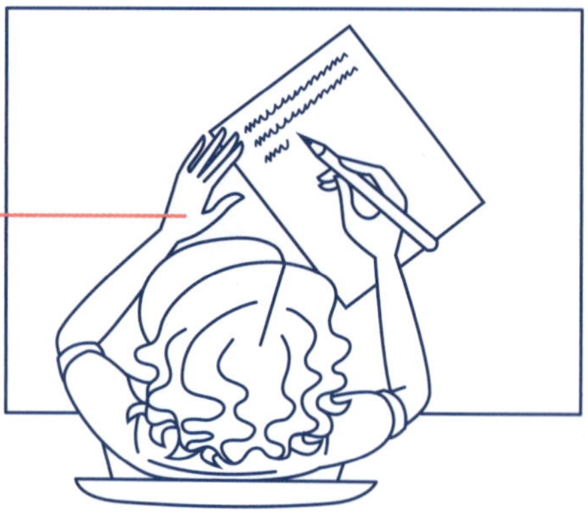

left-handed

right-handed

Pencil grip

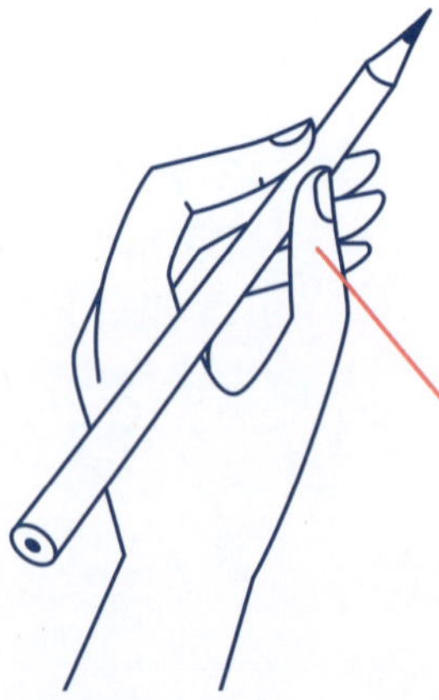

Hold your pencil with one finger on top of the barrel.

Support the barrel with your thumb.

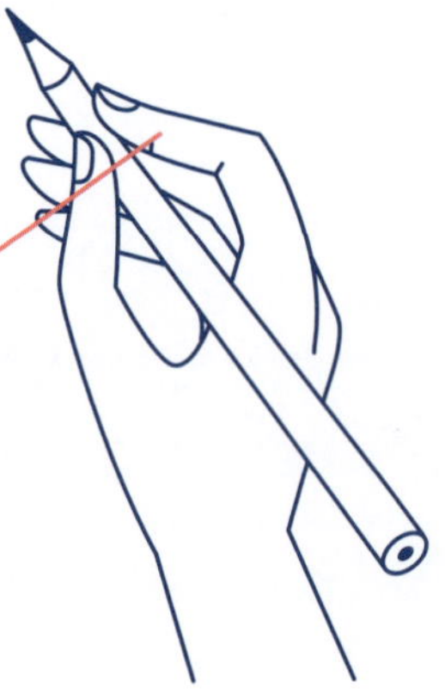

left-handed

right-handed

Patterning exercises

Trace and copy the patterns. Complete the rows.

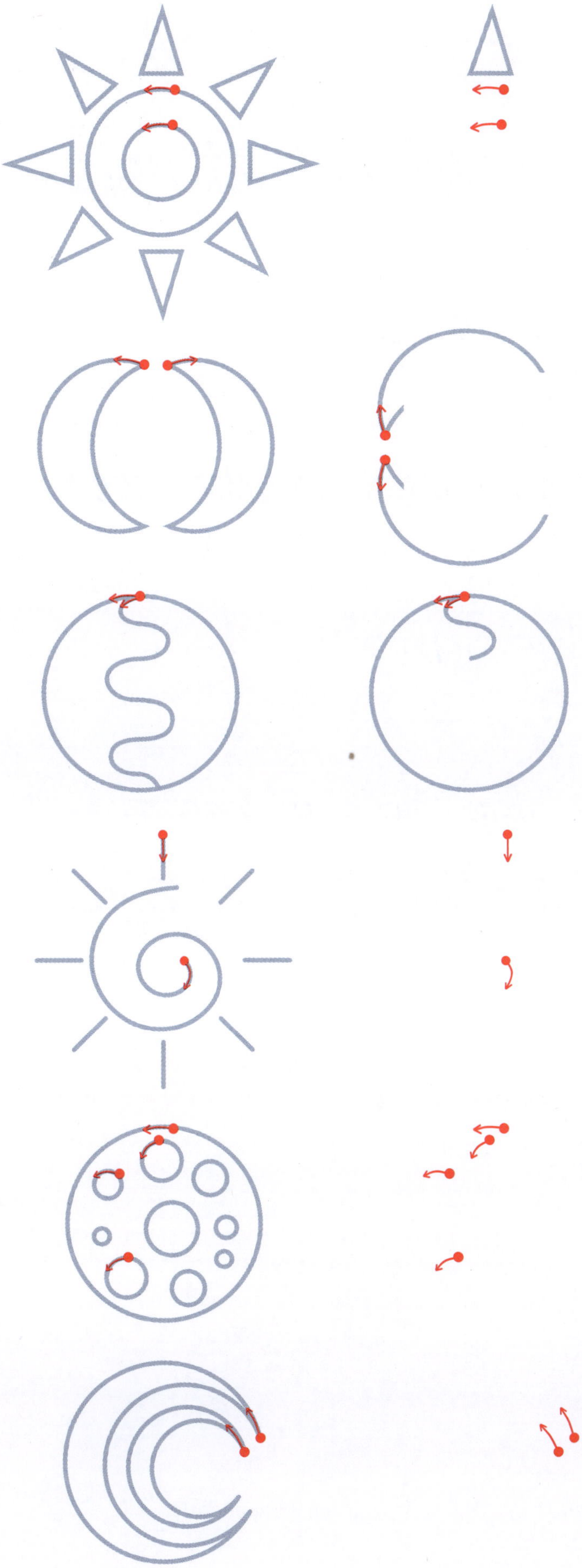

Print script

Revise your print script. Match a word to its meaning, then copy the text.

hydrogen   stars   orbits

__________: astronomical bodies that are visible at night and are not planets

__________: the paths Earth and other planets take around the Sun

__________: the gas the Sun is mostly made up of

Self-assessment

My print script is:

☐ good.

☐ very good.

☐ excellent!

Capital letters

Revise your capital letters.

A B C D E F G H I J K L M N O P

Q R S T U V W X Y Z

Copy the words using all capital letters.

ENERGY ATMOSPHERE

UNIVERSE SOLAR LUNAR

ECLIPSE ROTATE GRAVITY

Rewrite these words in all capital letters.

asteroid comet telescope

satellites terrestrial moon

equinox elliptical transit

Labelling diagrams

Finish labelling the lunar cycle diagram with words from the box. Use print script.

full Moon	first quarter	waxing gibbous
waning crescent	waxing crescent	

Clue: 'waning' means less and less of the Moon's surface is illuminated by the Sun's light.

The lunar cycle

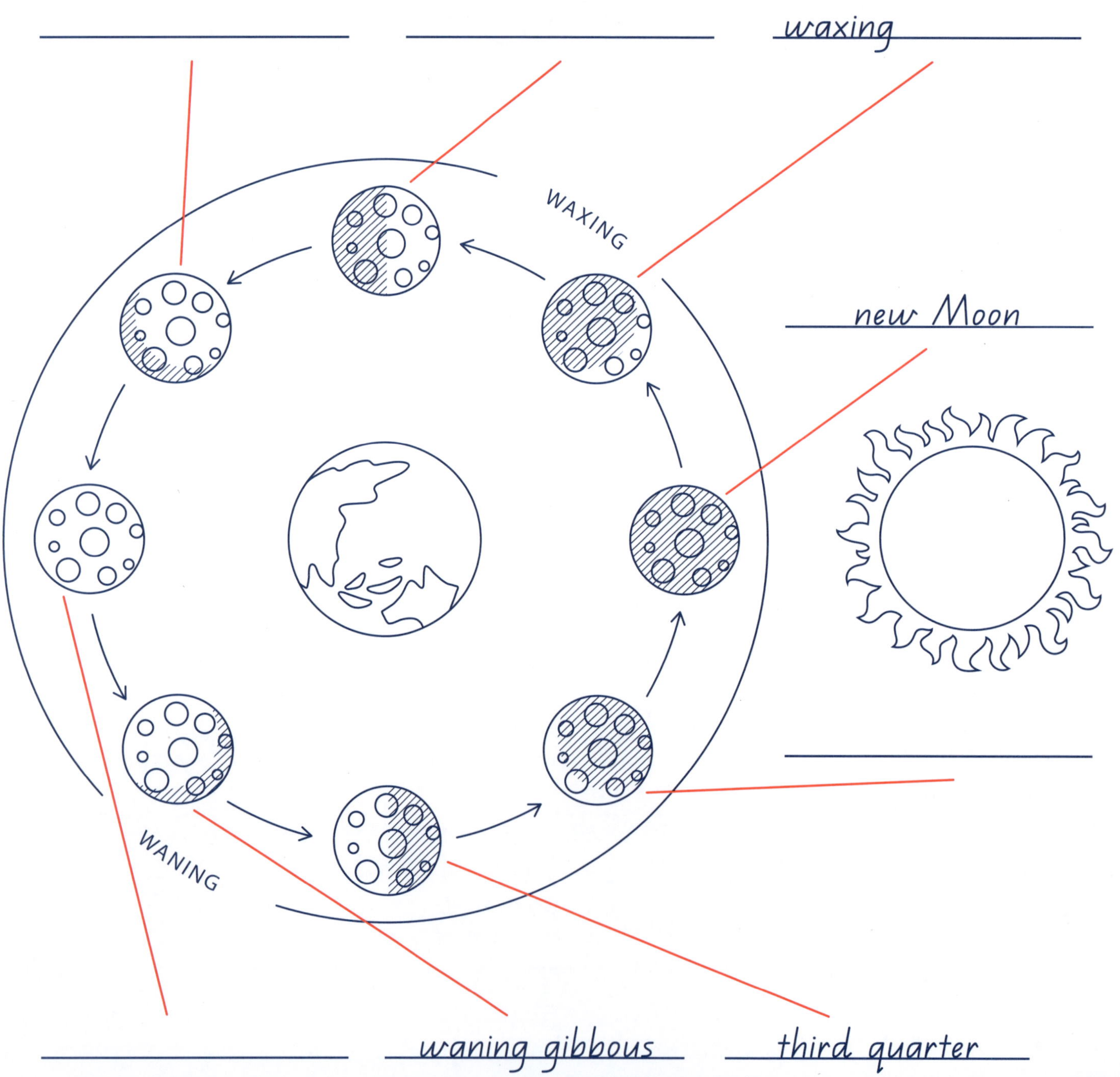

Numerals

Revise your numerals. Write the missing numerals in the gaps, then copy the text. get.ga/PMWA120

Earth is one hundred and fifty

million kilometres from the Sun.

= ______________ km

The circumference of Earth is forty

thousand and thirty kilometres.

= ___________ km

It takes three hundred and

sixty-five days for Earth to orbit

the Sun.

= ________ days

The letter 'x'

ax xe

Practise the steps for the word 'axis', then copy the other 'x' words.

1 av 2 ax 3 axis

apex axed boxes exact deluxe

reflex waxing exclaim expert

index sixteen texture excuse

excite export extinct relax

Copy these patterns to practise 'x' joins.

axa exe ixi

xox xux xtx

Joining from 'o'

oo on

TIP The letter 'o' starts and finishes at the top middle position.

Practise the steps for the word 'moon'.

1 mo 2 mo 3 moo 4 moon

Practise diagonal joins to 'o'.

lost comical notable lose home

Practise horizontal joins to 'o'.

cross grown rode worn roar

Practise joins from 'o' to head and body letters.

obvious books bottle off hollow

Try some more double 'o' words.

afternoon bedroom kangaroos roof

swoop woollen goose hooked foot

The letter 'f'

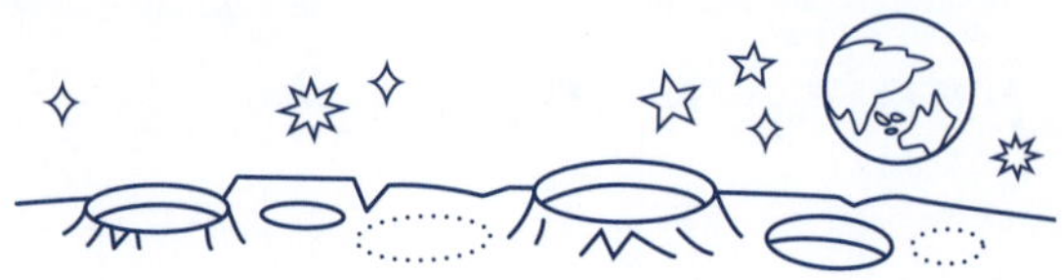

Practise writing 'f' at the beginning of a word.
Use the crossbar to join to the next letter.

flare freeze fumble faint fabric

failure focus flexible famine

Practise writing the modified 'f' used when there is a join to 'f'.

beliefs perform unsafe reflex wolf

wonderful afterwards awfully

Practise writing words containing double 'f'.

difficult fluffy sufficient offline

offering offshore efficient graffiti

Copy these patterns to practise 'f' joins.

fff fff ofof afaf

Slope

Consistent slope helps legibility.

Slope lines can be drawn on the vertical parts of a letter.
Complete the slope lines with your ruler.

m t a d f p n r q u

Now, rewrite the letters above against the slope lines provided.

m

Copy the text, then draw in slope lines.

Eight planets orbit the Sun. Our planet rotates on its axis as it orbits. One rotation takes 24 hours. For the side of Earth facing the Sun, it is daytime. The Sun appears to move across the sky as the day passes.

Spacing

Rewrite the text with even spacing between letters and words.

get.ga/PMWA121

O ur E arth s pins tilted at
an angle on its ax is.

Copy the text, then add the letter 'o' between each word to assess your spacing.

TheotiltoofoEarth is what causes
our seasons. In summer, more
sunlight reaches us as our
hemisphere tilts towards the Sun.

Self-assessment

My spacing looks:

☐ inconsistent.

☐ consistent.

Speed

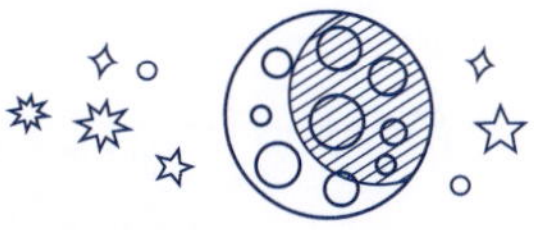

Work with a partner. How many times can you write the same word in one minute?

Print

moon

_____ times

Cursive

moon

_____ times

Capital letters

MOON

_____ times

Which script is your most legible? ______________________________

End-of-module evaluation: A flat Earth?

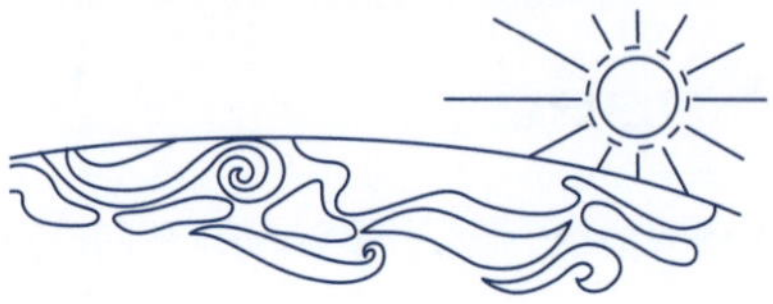

Copy the text, then evaluate your handwriting.

Today, we know that Earth is spherical, but there was a time when it was believed to be flat. Many early maps depict a flat Earth. From our everyday view, Earth looks flat. However, the view of our planet from space gives us a more accurate idea.

Evaluation grid				
	Student		Teacher	
Letters and words are a consistent size.	☐ Yes	☐ No	☐ Yes	☐ No
Letters and words are evenly spaced.	☐ Yes	☐ No	☐ Yes	☐ No
Slope is consistent.	☐ Yes	☐ No	☐ Yes	☐ No
All joins are accurate.	☐ Yes	☐ No	☐ Yes	☐ No
Handwriting is legible.	☐ Yes	☐ No	☐ Yes	☐ No

Introducing 8 mm blue lines

TIP As your handwriting improves, you can progress to smaller blue writing lines.

Copy the text.

An ascender is the part of a head and body letter that extends up towards the line above it. The letters b, d, h, k, l and t have ascenders. A descender is the part of a body and tail letter that extends below the baseline. The letters g, j, p, q, y and z have descenders. The letter f has both an ascender and a descender.

TIP When writing on smaller blue lines, don't crash!

✗
stopping
crashing

✓
stopping
crashing

Copy the text.

To help avoid letters on different lines crashing into each other, ascenders should only extend two-thirds of the way to the line above, and descenders should only fall one-third of the way to the line below.

Patterning exercises

Trace and complete the patterns.

Print script

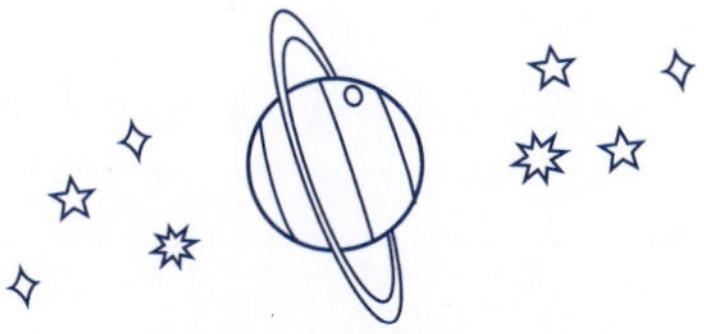

Revise the print alphabet.

a b c d e f g h i j k l m n o p q r s t u v w x y z

Copy these words in print script.

Ceres dwarf planet asteroid belt inner craters

Use the words above to complete the sentences. Then copy the text.

Ceres is a ________ ________. It is located in the

________ ________ between Mars and Jupiter.

________ is covered in many small ________. It is

the only dwarf planet in the ________ solar system.

Copy the facts about dwarf planets. Use print script.

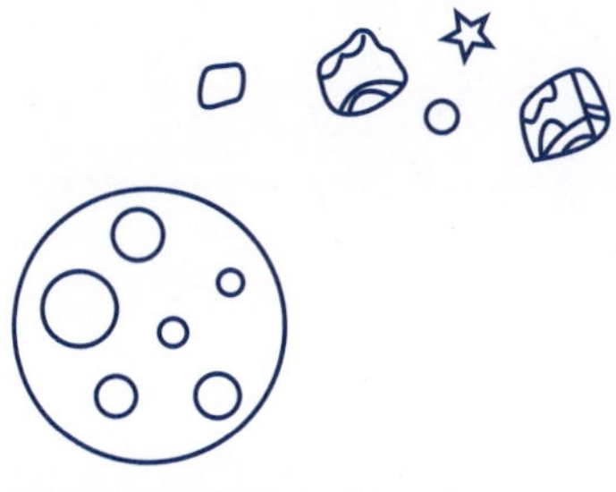

Dwarf planets are smaller than planets.

They are rounded objects that orbit the Sun.

They are not moons.

Pluto is a dwarf planet.

Converting between scripts

Complete the table to practise print, cursive and capital letters.

Print	Cursive	Capital letters
Milky Way	Milky Way	
		UNIVERSE
solar system		
	planets	
Mercury		
	Venus	
Mars		
	asteroids	
Kuiper belt		
	satellites	
meteoroid		
	Earth	

Match each definition to a word from the table above. Write the answer in your preferred script.

- the red planet made up of dense rock: ______________________
- the galaxy that contains our solar system: ______________________
- a belt of small bodies beyond Neptune: ______________________
- spacecraft or astronomical bodies in orbit: ______________________
- the only planet known to support human life: ______________________
- the planet closest to the Sun: ______________________

Labelling diagrams

Label the planets in our solar system. Use print script.

Earth	Venus	Mercury	Uranus
Saturn	Jupiter	Mars	Neptune

The planets of our solar system

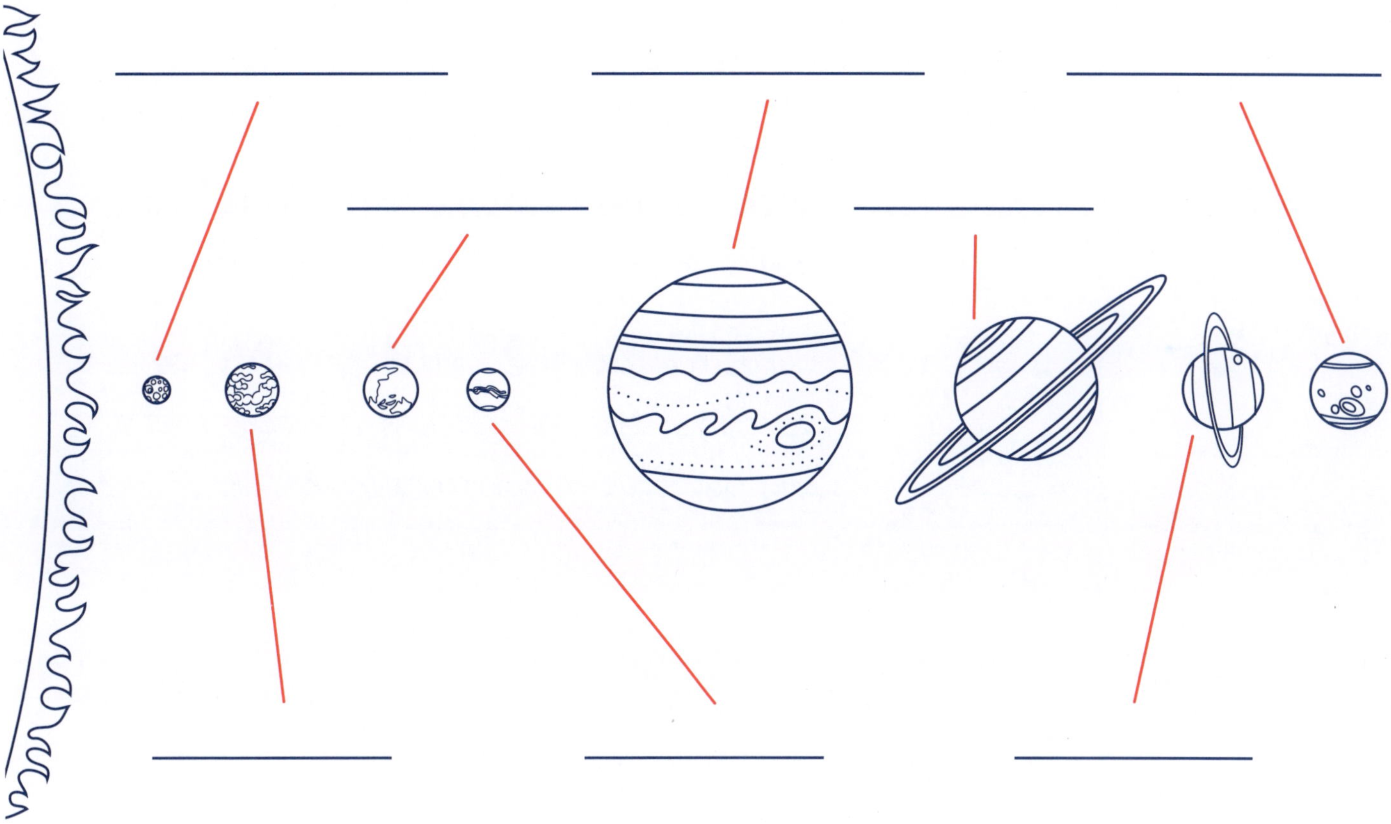

Now, write the names of the planets in cursive, starting with the planet closest to the Sun.

Self-assessment

My print script is:

☐ good.

☐ very good.

☐ out of this world!

Numerals

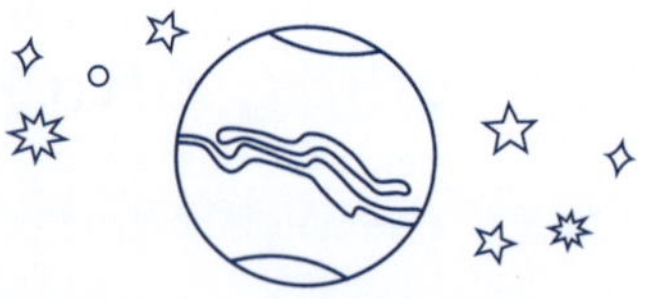

Add the missing numerals and numeral names in the table below.

Planet	Diameter	Diameter in words
Mercury	4 879 km	Four thousand, eight hundred and seventy-nine kilometres
Venus		Twelve thousand, one hundred and four kilometres
Earth	12 756 km	
Mars		Six thousand, seven hundred and ninety-two kilometres
Jupiter		One hundred and forty-two thousand, nine hundred and eighty-four kilometres
Saturn	120 536 km	
Uranus	51 118 km	
Neptune		Forty-nine thousand, five hundred and twenty-eight kilometres

Which planet is the largest? ______________________

Which planet is the smallest? ______________________

Which planet is most similar in size to Earth? ______________________

List the planets from smallest to largest. ______________________

____

Drop-on joins

la

Take the exit of 'l' high, lift your pencil and drop on 'a', starting 'a' by sliding horizontally.

Practise the steps for the word 'solar'.

1 sol   2 solar

Practise dropping on the shoulder letters a, c, d, g and q in the words below. The dots show where the drop-on joins are.

get.ga/PMWA122

planets galaxy magnetic metallic mantle

heat rotate clouds degrees volcanoes asteroids

rotational terrestrial eclipse launch equal

Add dots to indicate where there would be drop-on joins when writing in cursive.

astronaut lunar starlight meteoroid waxing

magnitude black hole elliptical mass radiation

Prove your dots were placed correctly by writing the words in cursive.

Self-assessment

My use of drop-on joins:

☐ needs more practice.

☐ is getting there.

☐ is good.

ISBN: 9780170403917

The letter 's'

Copy these words with print 's'.

solar system scientific eclipse sky supernova

spectrum surface smaller storm shower

synergy superior stratosphere shooting star

Copy these words with modified 's'. The join to 's' is diagonal.

astronomer phase cluster crescent density

dust planets giants Uranus moons

debris gas sustain acclimatise rotates

Copy these words with horizontal joins to 's'.

Mars appears close doors post most

cosmic expose position costume gears

purpose officers atmosphere sparse thermostat

Now, copy these words with double 's'.

discussion mass pressure compress across

airless assembled necessary boundless formless

closeness countless massive emission classify

Top finishers and the letter 'e'

o r v w

Top finishing letters do not join to 'e'. Copy these words, then underline those letter pairs.

discovered three very travel pressure coexist

extreme nowhere rest powerful adventurer

current drive over observed active explore

Rewrite these words in cursive.

region recently arrived several atmosphere

hemisphere structure interest average echoes

Copy the text.

Jupiter is the largest planet in the solar system.

Its stripes are made up of ammonia and water.

Astronomers believe it might have up to 67 moons.

Because it is made up of swirling gases and liquid,

Jupiter does not have a solid surface.

ISBN: 9780170403917

Slope

Test your slope. Copy these words within the parallel lines, then draw in slope lines.

red

Mars

craters

Rewrite the words, using the slope lines as a guide.

dust storms   iron oxide   polar ice caps   planet

Self-assessment

My slope is:

☐ inconsistent.

☐ mostly consistent.

☐ consistent.

Spacing

Read the sentence below, then write it with even spacing between letters and words.

Cons istent sp ac ing betw een le tters an d word s

makes y ou r handwr iting eas ier to r ead.

Write each word in the word shapes below. If your letter spacing is even, the word will fit in the shape.

dwarf

temperature

comets

surface

distance

asteroids

Copy the text, then add the letter 'o' between words to assess your spacing.

Whenotheosolar system was formed, the leftover material

became asteroids, meteoroids and comets. These travel

around, or orbit, the Sun. A meteor, or shooting star, is a

meteoroid that enters Earth's atmosphere and burns up.

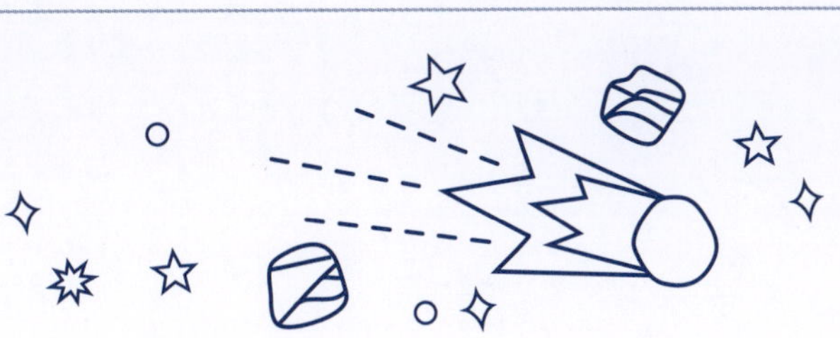

Size

How much does your handwriting vary in size from the models?
Copy these words in the spaces provided.

speeds travel gravity energy temperature

atmosphere galaxy moons satellites particles

spiral debris spacecraft formation motion

Sometimes you need to write at a different size. Can you change the size of your writing and maintain your legibility?

space space space space space

Write the word 'Mars' in cursive in the word shapes below. Use the shapes to help you write at a consistent size.

Mars

get.ga/PMWA123

Speed

Work with a partner. How many times can you write the word 'orbit' in one minute?

Print

orbit

_____ times

Cursive

orbit

_____ times

Capital letters

ORBIT

_____ times

Which script did you write the quickest?

print   cursive   CAPITAL LETTERS

Which script did you write the neatest?

print   cursive   CAPITAL LETTERS

ISBN: 9780170403917

End-of-module evaluation: Saturn's rings

Copy the text, than evaluate your handwriting.

Saturn, like the other gas giants, Jupiter, Uranus and Neptune, is surrounded by rings. Saturn's rings are very bright and contain lots of material. The rings are actually made up of thousands of ringlets. The band of rings is up to 282 000 km across, but only 1 km thick. The dusty ice particles that make up the rings vary in size from grains to boulders. Scientists have been using the Hubble Space Telescope to take pictures of the rings in the hope that we can learn more about them.

Evaluation grid				
	Student		Teacher	
Letters and words are a consistent size.	☐ Yes	☐ No	☐ Yes	☐ No
Letters and words are evenly spaced.	☐ Yes	☐ No	☐ Yes	☐ No
Slope is consistent.	☐ Yes	☐ No	☐ Yes	☐ No
All joins are accurate.	☐ Yes	☐ No	☐ Yes	☐ No
Handwriting is legible.	☐ Yes	☐ No	☐ Yes	☐ No

ISBN: 9780170403917

Patterning exercises

Trace and complete each pattern.

ISBN: 9780170403917

Print script

Astronauts have daily routines, just like you. Copy these routines in print script.

wash hair *brush teeth* *use bathroom* *go to sleep*

perform experiments *exercise* *enjoy leisure activities*

eat food *call or email family* *read a book*

Each of the routines above starts with a verb. Write the verbs in print script.

Design a daily menu for an astronaut on a space mission using items from the box below. Use print script.

brownies fruit macaroni and cheese spaghetti
tomato sauce yogurt mustard oatmeal
nuts peanut butter chicken beef seafood
coffee tea fruit juice lemonade tortillas

Breakfast:

Lunch:

Dinner:

ISBN: 9780170403917

Capital letters

Revise your capital letters.

A B C D E F G H I J K L M N O P

Q R S T U V W X Y Z

Rewrite these words in all capital letters.

living working space food clothing
exercise communicate research zero gravity
self-care daily mission dreams snoring
excitement motion nightmares wake hours

List the capital letters in the words above that have downstrokes.

List the capital letters in the words above that have a rounded shape.

List the capital letters in the words above that have diagonal lines.

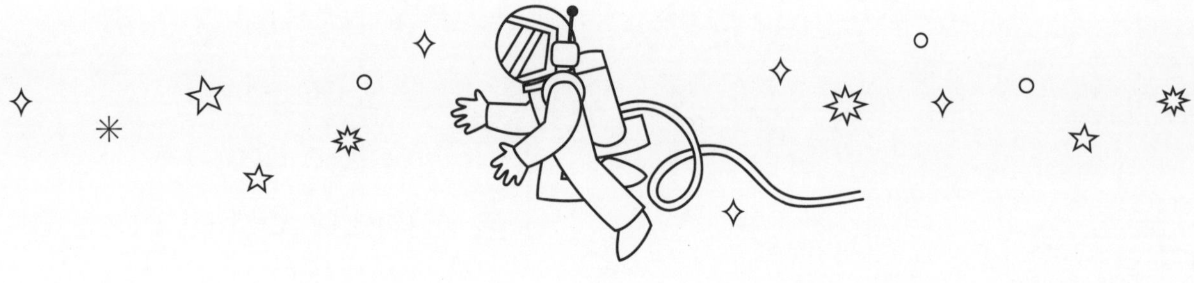

ISBN: 9780170403917

Labelling diagrams

Label the parts of a space shuttle. Use print script.

A NASA space shuttle

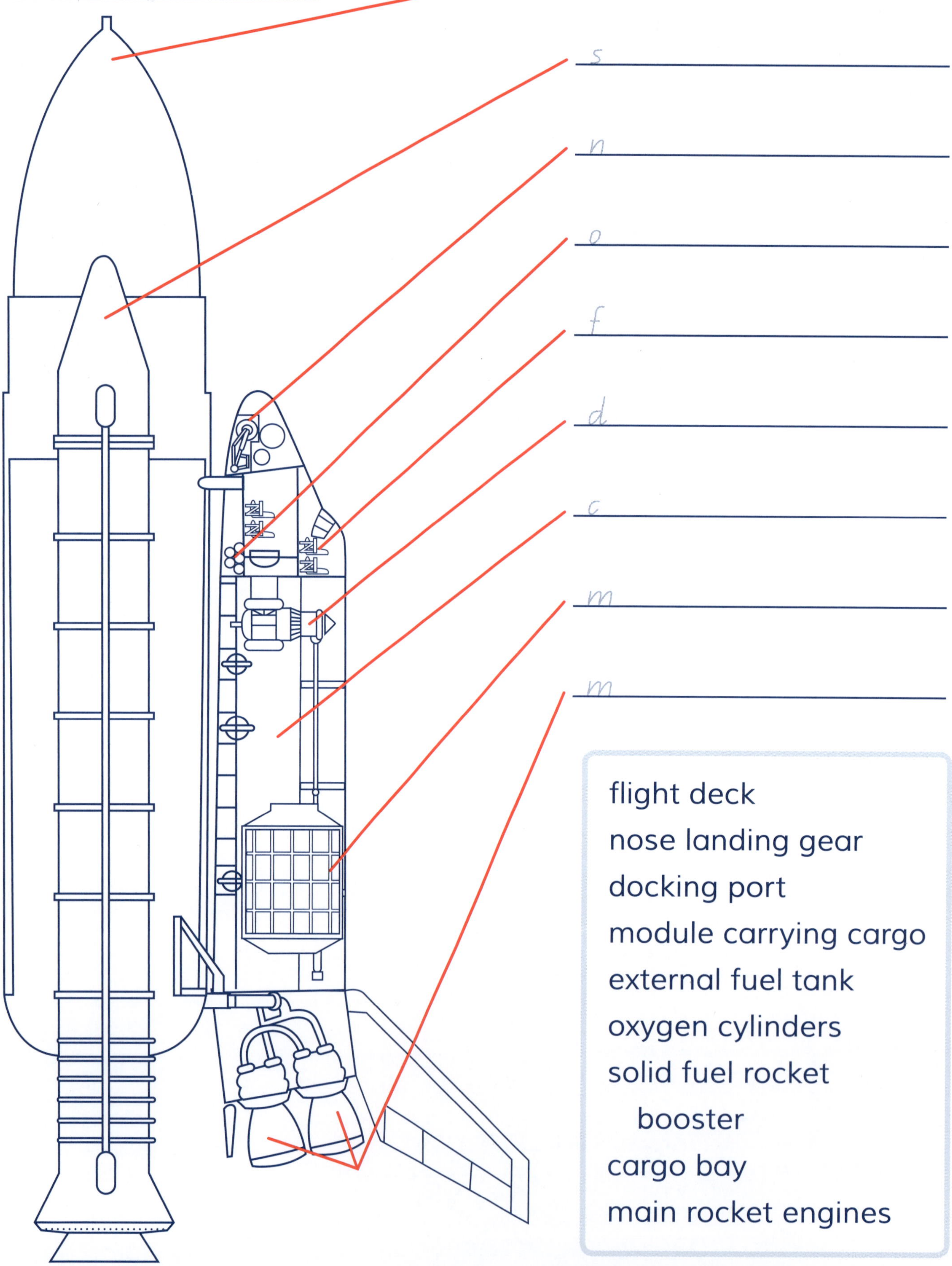

flight deck
nose landing gear
docking port
module carrying cargo
external fuel tank
oxygen cylinders
solid fuel rocket booster
cargo bay
main rocket engines

Numerals

Fill in the blanks, then copy these numerals and numeral names using cursive.

7 seven

70 seventy

700 ______ hundred

7000 ______ thousand

70 000 ______ thousand

700 000 ______ hundred thousand

7 000 000 ______ million

Write each numeral in words.

6 six

60 sixty

600

6000

60 000

600 000

6 000 000

5 five

50 fifty

500

5000

50 000

500 000

5 000 000

Use words to write the speed of light in metres per second. It is written as a numeral below.

299 792 458

ISBN: 9780170403917

Practising diagonal joins

Take a letter from each box to make letter pairs with diagonal joins.

a c d e h i k l m n t u

to

b e g h i k l m n t u y z

Copy the phrases, then underline the diagonal joins.

International Space Station unique place

six people live occupied since November 2000

conduct research solar arrays provide power

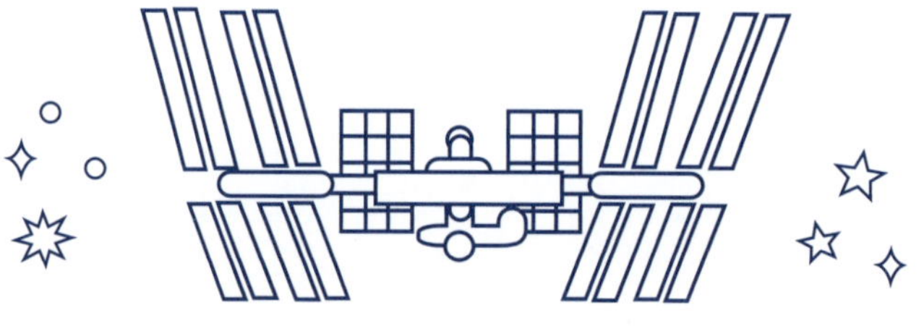

Make new words by adding a letter or letters to these word endings with diagonal joins.

____ake ____ain ____ate ____ill ____oke

____ait ____ail ____ink ____ent

ISBN: 9780170403917

Practising horizontal joins

Take a letter from each box to make letter pairs with horizontal joins.
Remember not to dip the join too far.

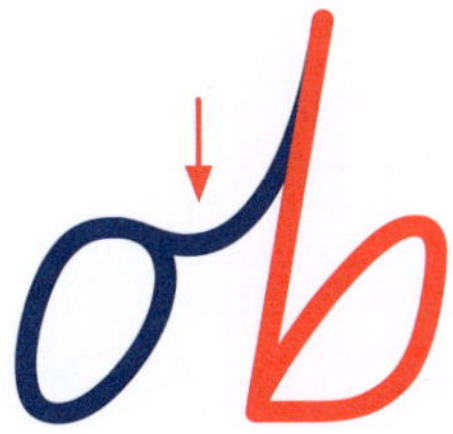

o r v w

to

a b c d g h i k l m n o p
r s t u x y z

Copy the words, then underline the horizontal joins.

get.ga/PMWA124

clothes astronaut formal outside move

around protects dangers several ways

oxygen water sound dangerous moving

covers possible cooling during primary

Make new words by adding a letter or letters to these word endings with horizontal joins.

___oat ___og ___orn ___ood ___ook ___oot

___ork ___oon ___one ___ost ___oor

ISBN: 9780170403917

Writing the letter 'r'

r r or r r

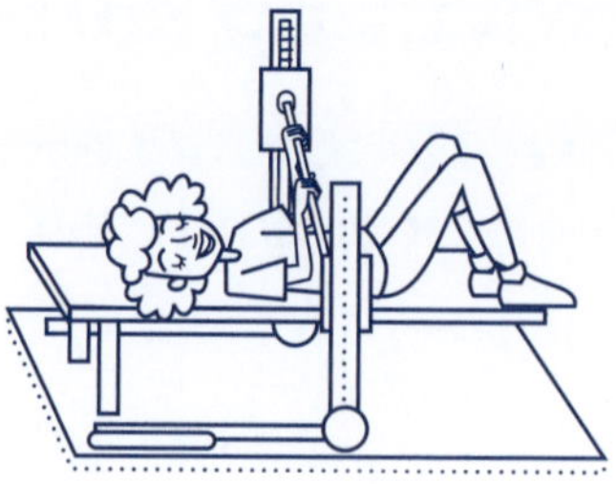

The letter 'r' can be joined to the next letter or you can leave it unjoined. Whether or not you join is a personal choice.

Copy the following words with 'r' joined and not joined. Circle the word in each pair that you found more comfortable to write.

personal personal *rigorous rigorous* *revolve revolve*

hurry hurry *restraints restraints* *orbit orbit*

work work *orientation orientation* *radio radio*

permanent permanent *exercise exercise*

Copy these patterns to practise your 'r' joins.

rnrn riri rrrr rara

urur oror mrmr crcr

ISBN: 9780170403917

Slope

Try copying the letter 'm' on slope lines at different angles.

0 degrees	10 degrees	20 degrees	30 degrees
mmm	mmm	mmm	mmm

Circle the version that is closest to your natural slope.

Copy the sentence below, then draw in slope lines using a ruler.

Earth's moon is a natural satellite.

Trace and copy these patterns in parallel lines. Try to maintain a consistent slope.

ono ele uu

Self-assessment

My slope is:

☐ inconsistent.

☐ mostly consistent.

☐ consistent.

ISBN: 9780170403917

Spacing

Look at the different versions of the word 'revolve'. Circle the version that has the most appropriate letter spacing.

revolve revolve revolve

Copy the text, then add an 'o' between each word to check your spacing.

Astronauts,olikeous,oaim to get eight hours of sleep
while in space. They sleep in sleeping bags in their own
crew cabin. The sleeping bags are attached to part of
the spacecraft so the astronauts don't float around
while sleeping in the microgravity of space.

Did you fit the same number of words on each line as the model sentences? Circle.

YES NO

Self-assessment

My spacing is:

☐ getting there.

☐ good.

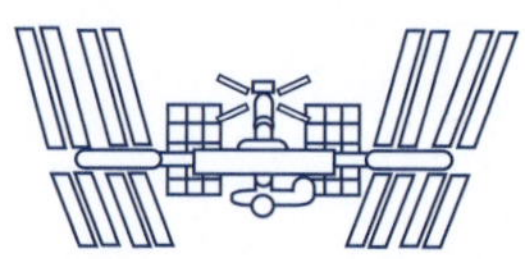

☐ excellent!

ISBN: 9780170403917

Size

Trace and complete these patterns and words at different sizes.
Try to maintain a consistent slope.

launch launch launch

ISBN: 9780170403917

Speed and legibility

It is important to balance speed and accurate letter formation so your writing is quick and legible.

Work with a partner to find out how many times you can write the word 'astronaut' in cursive in one minute.

get.ga/PMWA125

astronaut

____ times

Now write the word again. This time, write as neatly as you can. How many times did you write it in one minute?

astronaut

____ times

Now find out how many times you can write the word neatly in print script in one minute.

astronaut

____ times

Did you write it more times in one minute than in cursive, or fewer times? MORE FEWER

ISBN: 9780170403917

End-of-module evaluation: Experimenting with gravity

Copy the text, then evaluate your handwriting. Try the experiment with a partner.

Goal *To test how gravity affects an object's speed*

Materials *pencil and paper*

stack of books of a similar size

piece of craft wood toy car stopwatch

Steps

1. Draw up a table for recording data.

2. Set up a ramp by placing books under one end of the craft wood.

3. Place the toy car at the top of the ramp. Record the time taken for the car to reach the end of the ramp.

4. Repeat, increasing the height of the ramp each time.

Conclusion How did the steepness of the ramp affect the speed of the car? Discuss your conclusions about gravity with your partner.

Evaluation grid				
	Student		Teacher	
Letters and words are a consistent size.	☐ Yes	☐ No	☐ Yes	☐ No
Letters and words are evenly spaced.	☐ Yes	☐ No	☐ Yes	☐ No
Slope is consistent.	☐ Yes	☐ No	☐ Yes	☐ No
All joins are accurate.	☐ Yes	☐ No	☐ Yes	☐ No
Handwriting is legible.	☐ Yes	☐ No	☐ Yes	☐ No

ISBN: 9780170403917

Patterning exercises

Complete the patterns.

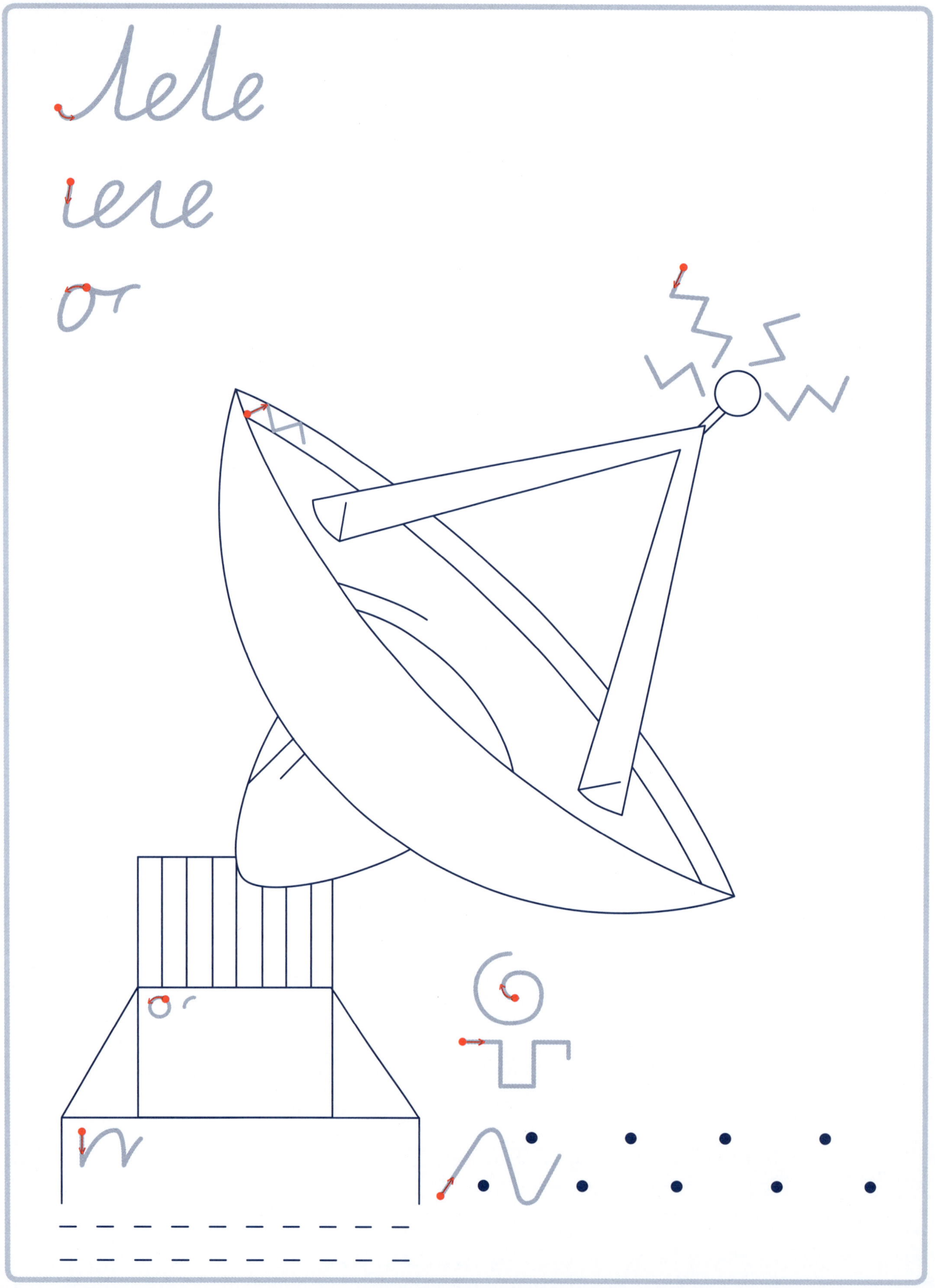

ISBN: 9780170403917

Print script

Add labels from the box to the timeline below.

1969	First human on the moon
1961	First human spaceflight
1971	First space probe to orbit Mars
1963	First woman in space
1957	First animal in orbit (Laika the dog)

A timeline of early space exploration

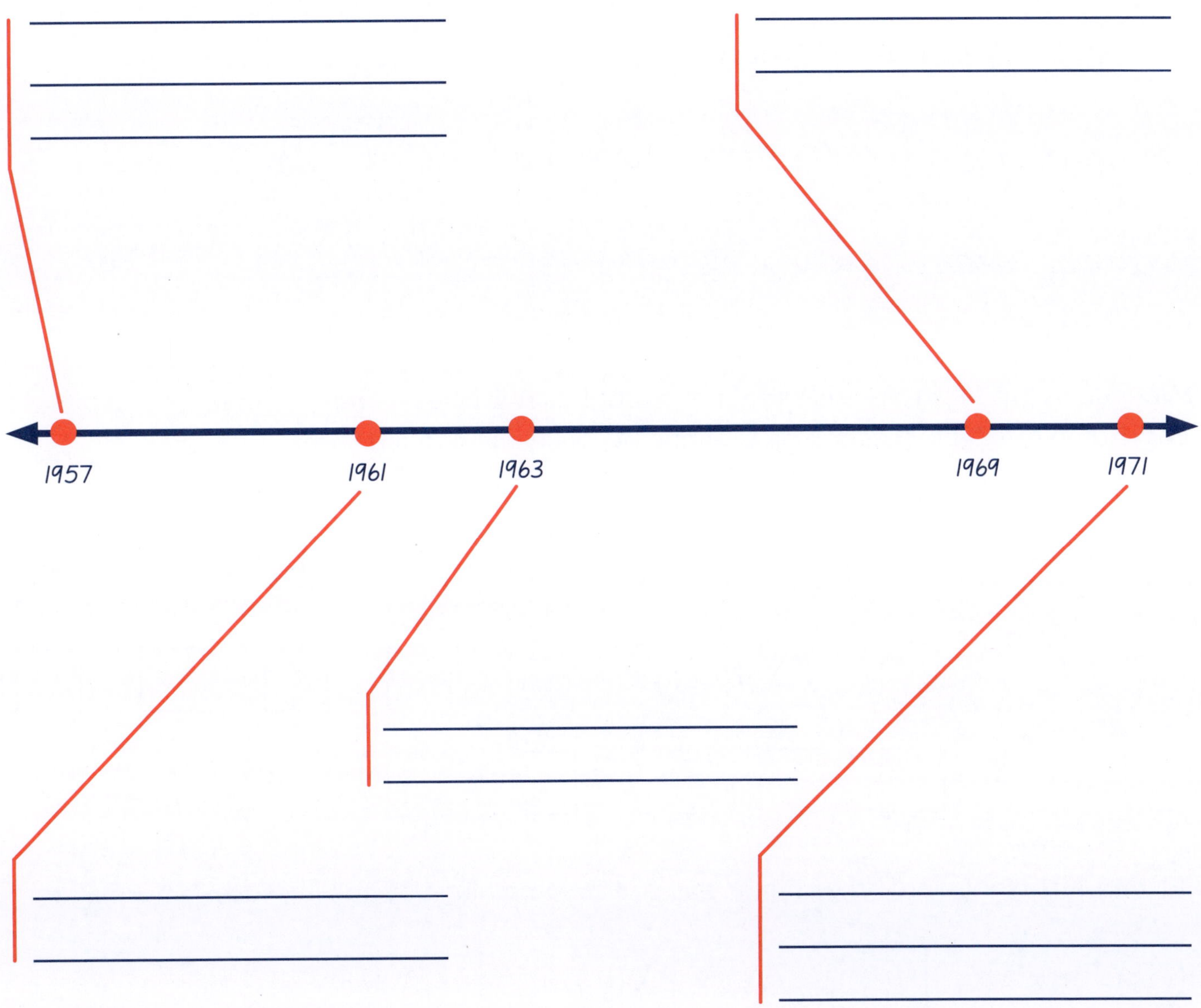

ISBN: 9780170403917

Capital letters

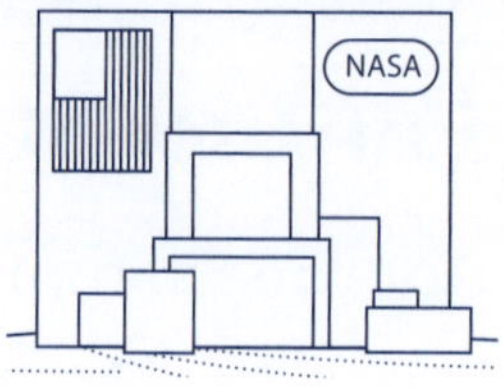

Rewrite each sentence in print, using capital letters in the correct places.

in 1963, the ussr launched the first female

astronaut, valentina tereshkova, into space.

nasa (national aeronautics and space administration),

the esa (european space agency) and csa

(canadian space agency) have collaborated to create

the james webb space telescope.

the first iss module launched was called 'zarya',

which means 'dawn' in russian.

Write each capital letter inside the shape that best matches its basic shape. For example, 'G' matches the circle shape because it is a round letter.

A E F G H I K L N O Q T U V X Y Z

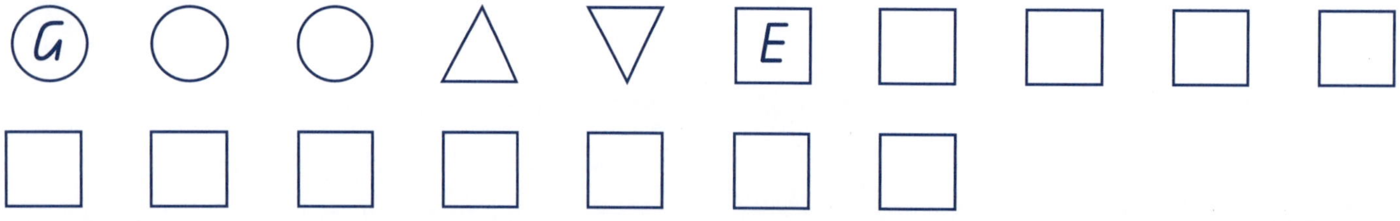

Just for fun, what word do you think this is? It's something you see in space.

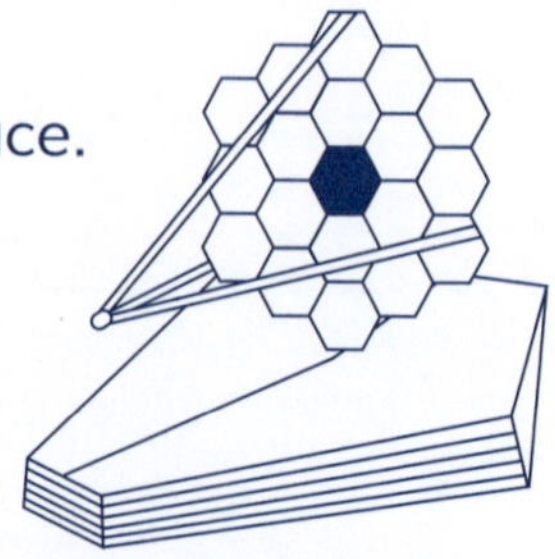

James Webb Space Telescope

ISBN: 9780170403917

Labelling diagrams

Label the parts of the Mars Curiosity Rover. Use print script.

wheels	Mars Curiosity Rover	turret
arm	body	power source	cameras

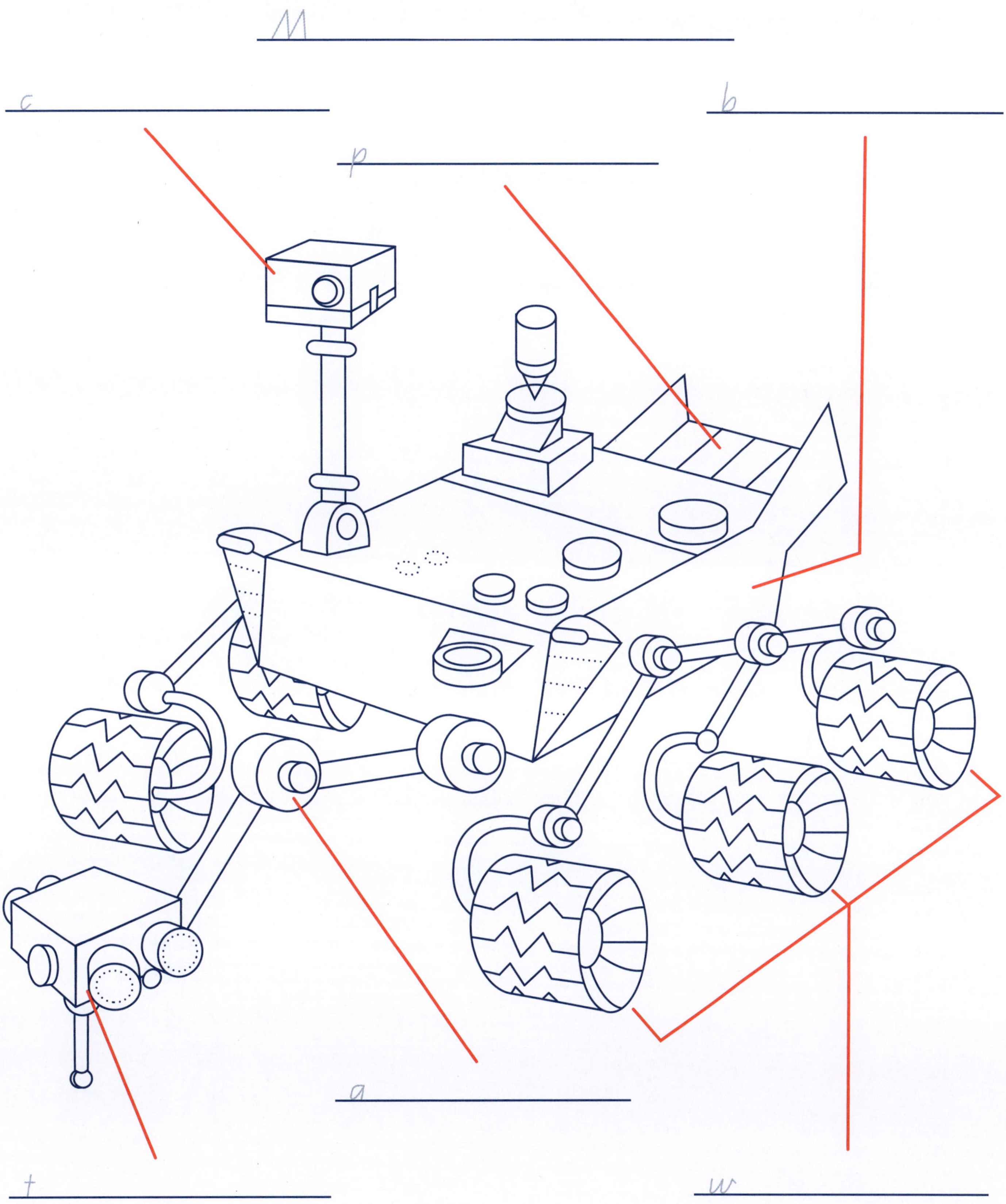

ISBN: 9780170403917

Numerals

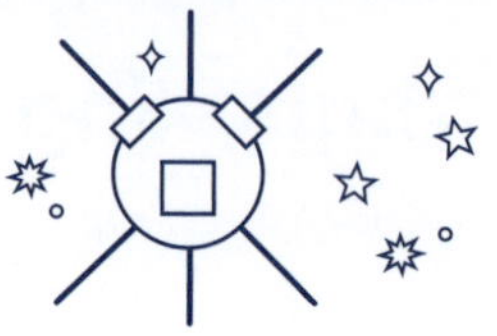

Can you write the following numerals and numeral names using this code?

 → 62 134

Sixty-two thousand, one hundred and thirty-four

 → ______

____

 → ______

____

 → ______

____

 → ______

____

Can you write codes for each of these numerals?

872 163

521 872

713 864

52 716

37 821

46 335

18 274

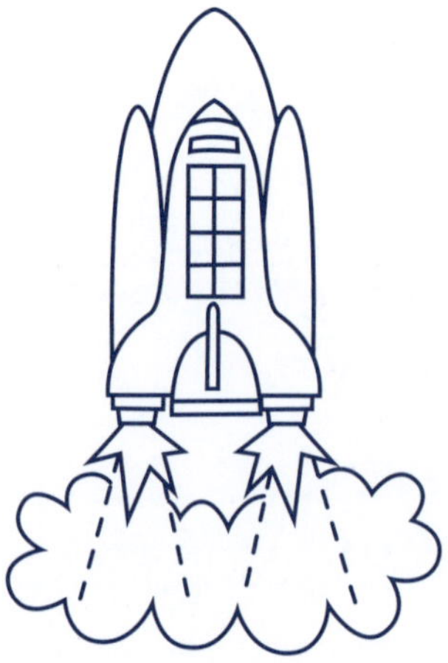

ISBN 9780170403917

Top finishers to ascenders

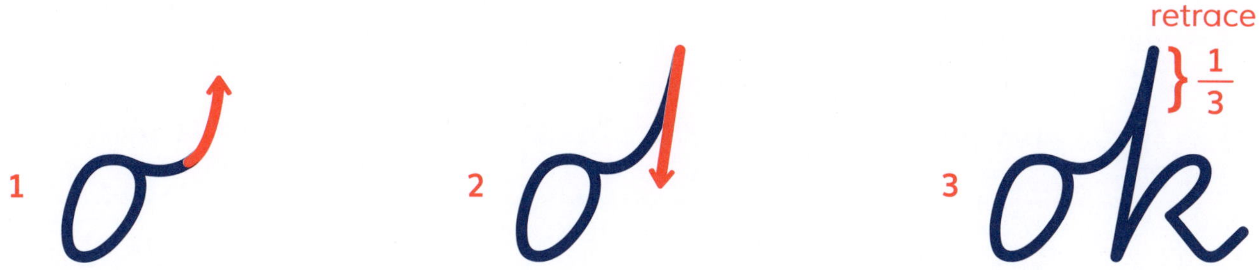

Remember: when joining a top finishing letter to an ascender, sweep up, then retrace about one-third.

Copy these letter pairs.

ob of oh ok ol ot rb rf rh rk rl rt

vl wh wl wt

Copy words using this join.

virtual technology objective whole revolve

solar turbulence violence volcanic pavlova

obscure observatory total starlight absolute

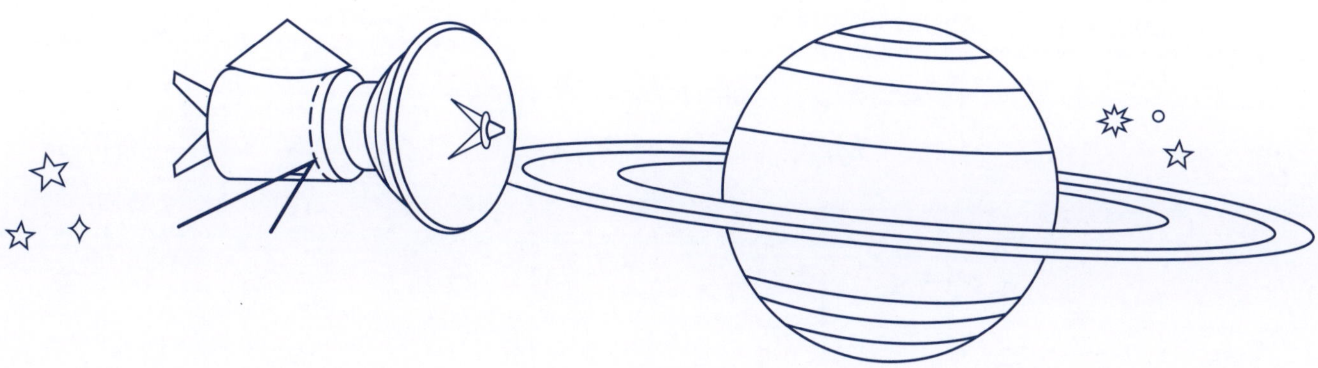

ISBN: 9780170403917

Revising the letter 'f'

Copy these words with open 'f'.

function bagful feature transfer forearm

flourish forwards factual satisfy fragile

freeze blissful ferocious transfix forage

Copy these words with modified 'f'.

clarify specify halfway painful perform careful

define afraid refined enforce briefly qualify

drafting dreadful infinite terrific inflated

Copy these words with double 'f'.

offend offset affair buffer afford officer

cliff buffet effect different effort sheriff

takeoff coffee suffix affirm muffle offence

Circle words that have an open 'f' when written in cursive, and underline words that have a modified 'f'.

furious facial modify cupful wolf outfit

frozen yourself forecast floating confuse doubtful

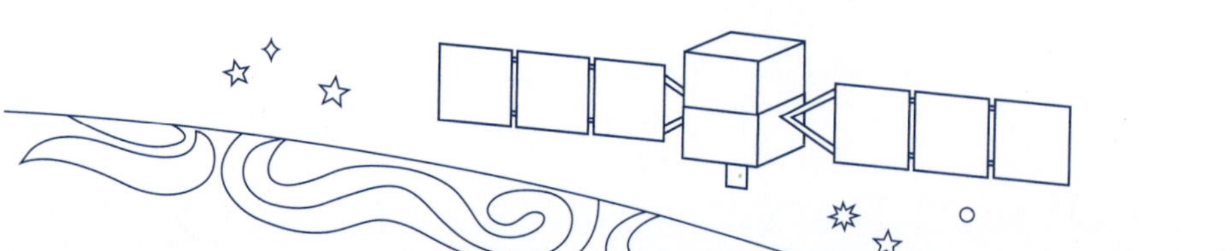

ISBN: 9780170403917

Classifying joins

Sort the following letter pairs into their correct join type.
Some letter pairs belong in more than one category.

cc ki ow wl vo ng rl co ac rs
ew wh ot cq om il nd ol cr on

Diagonal joins	Drop-on joins
Horizontal joins	**Top finishers to ascenders**

Rewrite this sentence in cursive four times.

The five boxing wizards jumped over the lazy frog.

List the letter pairs from the sentence above that join diagonally.

List the letter pairs from the sentence above with drop-on joins.

List the letter pairs from the sentence above that don't join.

ISBN: 9780170403917

Slope

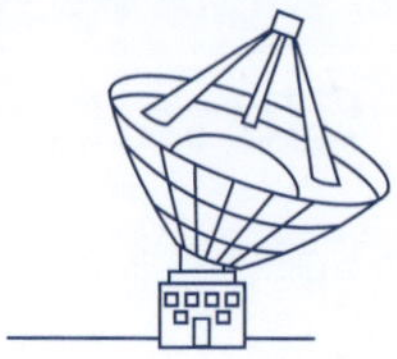

Practise maintaining a consistent slope. Copy each word in the slope grid.

exoplanet

universe

terrestrial

atmosphere

habitable

telescope

galaxy

Circle the statements that apply to you.

- These slope grids were easy to use.
- These slope grids were hard to use.
- These slope grids helped me make my slope consistent.

get.ga/PMWA126

Spacing

Copy the text, then check your spacing. Colour a small red square between each word.

The second planet from the Sun is Venus. Its surface temperature is 472°C. The size of Venus is similar to that of Earth. Venus has no moons or rings, and it rotates in the opposite direction to most other planets.

Copy these patterns to practise maintaining even spacing between letters.

ooo www eee

uuu mmm ulul

Look at the different versions of the word 'Neptune'. Circle the version that has the most appropriate letter spacing.

Neptune Neptune Neptune Neptune

Size

Trace and complete these patterns and words at different sizes. Try to maintain a consistent slope.

science

crater

elle ll

axis

>>>>

ox OX ox

Speed

Work with a partner to time how long it takes you to write the following text in each script.

> Neptune is a cold, dark planet with the strongest winds in the solar system. It is one of the gas giants, and the furthest planet from the Sun. Neptune has 13 known moons.

Print

____

____

____

____

______ minute(s) ______ seconds

Cursive

____

____

____

____

______ minute(s) ______ seconds

Which script did you write the quickest?

print *cursive*

Which script are you more comfortable writing?

print *cursive*

get.ga/PMWA127

Self-assessment

My legibility when writing at speed is:

☐ not bad.

☐ getting there.

☐ looking good!

End-of-module evaluation: The Hubble Space Telescope

Copy the text, then evaluate your handwriting.

The Hubble Space Telescope flies above Earth's atmosphere,

taking digital photographs like those you can take

with your mobile phone. It takes photographs of planets,

stars and galaxies, and sends them back to Earth

through radio waves. NASA launched the telescope

from the Kennedy Space Centre, Florida, USA, in 1990.

The Hubble Telescope orbits Earth at a speed of over

27 000 kilometres per hour.

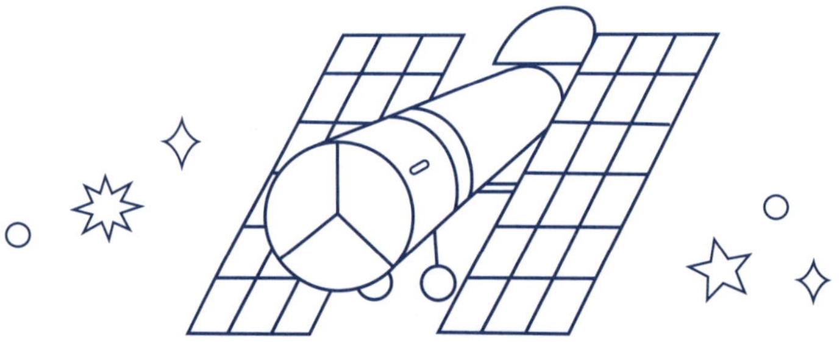

Evaluation grid				
	Student		Teacher	
Letters and words are a consistent size.	☐ Yes	☐ No	☐ Yes	☐ No
Letters and words are evenly spaced.	☐ Yes	☐ No	☐ Yes	☐ No
Slope is consistent.	☐ Yes	☐ No	☐ Yes	☐ No
All joins are accurate.	☐ Yes	☐ No	☐ Yes	☐ No
Handwriting is legible.	☐ Yes	☐ No	☐ Yes	☐ No

Introducing the flourished alphabet

The flourished alphabet is a decorative writing style. Use flourished letters for presentation purposes, or to help you develop your own unique handwriting style.

Try copying the flourished capital letters. Use the slope grids to guide you.

ISBN: 9780170403917

G G

H H

I I

J J

K K

L L

M M

N N

O O

P P

Q Q

R R

S S

T T

ISBN: 9780170403917

U U

V V

W W

1 2
X X

Y Y

Z Z

get.ga/PMWA128

Try writing the flourished lower-case letters.

a b

c d

e f

g h

i j

k l

m n

o p

q r

s t

u v

w x

y z

Circle the flourished letters that change from cursive, then copy the flourished alphabet.

a b c d e f g h i j k l m n o p q r s t u v
w x y z

Follow the steps below to write letter pairs in flourished script.

ab	1 a	2 ab	3 ab	ed	1 e	2 ed	3 ed
if	1 i	2 if	3 if	th	1 t	2 th	3 th
ok	1 o	2 ok	3 ok	il	1 i	2 il	
mp	1 m	2 mp	3 mp	ax	1 a	2 ax	

Using flourished script

Copy these entries for a glossary about space, using the flourished alphabet.

asteroids: rocky bodies smaller than planets, mostly found in a belt between Mars and Jupiter

comets: icy, dusty bodies that heat up when they orbit near the Sun, causing their ice to melt and creating a bright tail

eclipse: the phenomenon that occurs when one astronomical body cuts off the light of another

galaxy: a large group of stars bound together by gravity, such as the Milky Way galaxy that contains our solar system

meteoroids: rocky or metallic bodies that are smaller than asteroids; called meteors or shooting stars when they enter Earth's atmosphere and glow

Practising all scripts

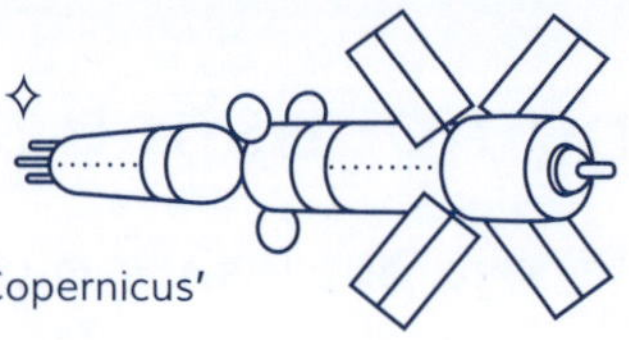
Mars Transfer Vehicle 'Copernicus'

Print script

a b c d e f g h i j k l m n o p q r s t u v w x y z

Queensland Modern Cursive

abcdefghijklmnopqrstuvwxyz

Capital letters

A B C D E F G H I J K L M N O P Q R S T U V

W X Y Z

Numerals

0 1 2 3 4 5 6 7 8 9

Flourished alphabet

aA bB cC dD eE fF gG

hH iI jJ kK lL mM

nN oO pP qQ rR sS tT

uU vV wW xX yY zZ

Independent writing activity

'Space exploration is good for humanity.'

Remember, a persuasive text must have:

- a title
- a statement of position
- a series of arguments
- a concluding statement.

Write a short persuasive text about why you agree or disagree with the statement above. Use your best cursive handwriting.

Teacher observation guide

Student is: left-handed ☐ right-handed ☐

Student demonstrates correct posture, paper position and pencil grip. ☐

Student forms the print alphabet with accuracy. ☐

Student forms capital letters with accuracy. ☐

Student can write numerals with accuracy. ☐

Student forms the following joins with accuracy:

- drop-on joins ☐
- diagonal joins ☐
- horizontal joins ☐
- 'x' joins ☐
- 'o' joins ☐
- 'f' joins ☐
- 's' joins ☐
- top finishers that do not join to 'e' ☐
- 'r' joins ☐

Student uses Queensland Modern Cursive confidently. ☐

Student can convert between scripts. ☐

Student uses 8 mm writing lines with accuracy. ☐

Student has an understanding of the factors that influence legibility (slope, spacing, size, speed). ☐

Student is progressing towards a fluent and legible personal handwriting style. ☐

Notes:

....

....

....

Date:

....